Common Sense
Engagement

Common Sense Engagement

Tom McQueen
with
Karl Horst

Xulon Press

Xulon Press
2301 Lucien Way #415
Maitland, FL 32751
407.339.4217
www.xulonpress.com

© 2017 by Tom McQueen with Karl Horst

All rights reserved solely by the author. The author guarantees all contents are original and do not infringe upon the legal rights of any other person or work. No part of this book may be reproduced in any form without the permission of the author. The views expressed in this

Printed in the United States of America.

ISBN-13: 9781545603956

Introduction

One of my favorite Chinese proverbs offers pretty sound advice for engaging employees in the workplace: *Tell me and I'll forget. Show me and I may remember. Involve me and I'll understand.*

Trustworthy research organizations studying the contemporary American workplace all report similar numbers:

✓ More than two-thirds of U.S. workers are not engaged at work.

✓ 89% of employers think their employees leave for more money; in fact, only 12% of employees actually do leave for more money.

✓ 75% of people voluntarily exiting their employment don't quit their jobs; they quit their bosses.

✓ 90% of leaders think an engagement strategy has an impact on business success, but barely 25% of them have a strategy.

✓ Companies with engaged employees earn 2.5 times more revenue than competitors with low engagement levels.

Corporations can create the best products and services, the loftiest business goals, and the best digital marketing strategies. And you know what? None of that matters if passionately engaged employees aren't driving their business engines.

Fortunately, achieving employee engagement isn't rocket science. Maybe that's the problem. American businesses seem to have overlooked the two foundational components of a common sense approach to creating energy and excitement among their workers.

Common Sense Engagement

When you've finished reading *Common Sense Engagement*, you will be able to create, customize, and follow a clear path to achieving higher levels of employee engagement resulting in unparalleled levels of success that will delight your co-workers, your customers, and your shareholders.

Tom McQueen
Vice President
It's Just Common Sense, LLC

Table of Contents

Introduction vii
The Caveat 1
Emotional Intelligence (EQ) 2
Coaching 15
The Employee Engagement Challenge 31
About the Authors 37

THE CAVEAT

In this book you're going to discover and be able to apply two foundational elements of a highly engaged workplace culture. But there's a caveat. Energy, excitement, enthusiasm, and engagement can never happen without having a solid plan for recruiting, selecting, hiring, and training the right people.

Getting the right people on the bus has to be more than a hope for finding some nice folks to work for you. Making bad hires is a mistake that can cost you big-time. In a Robert Half survey of CFO's throughout the country, 39% reported that lower staff morale is the biggest impact of a poor hiring decision. It's virtually impossible to have an engaged work group when morale is suffering. Furthermore, 34% of the CFO's also noted that the greatest cost of a bad hire is lost productivity.

Therefore, before initiating a plan to create or strengthen a highly engaged workplace, carefully examine your current personnel as well as your talent acquisition strategy. If what you discover is less than satisfactory, then let us help you develop a comprehensive and effective plan for finding the people that have the greatest potential to accomplish your business goals and objectives.

Once you have the right people in place, employ these two foundations of a highly engaged workforce...

Emotional Intelligence (EQ)

If your emotional abilities aren't in hand, if you don't have self-awareness, if you are not able to manage your distressing emotions, if you can't have empathy and have effective relationships, then no matter how smart you are, you are not going to get very far.

Daniel Goleman, Author
Emotional Intelligence

Without emotional intelligence, authentic employee engagement isn't happening. It's that simple.

If you're like most people, you probably know at least one highly intelligent and gifted person who was promoted to a leadership position at work, only to become a colossal failure. And you probably also know someone with better than average, though not exceptional, knowledge and technical skills who was similarly promoted to a leadership role in an organization and became highly successful.

Given the fact that there are different styles of leadership that can be equally effective, what causes one leader to succeed and another to fail? Volumes of contemporary research support the theory that understanding and employing the practical applications of *emotional intelligence* is the one critical component that all effective leaders have in common, despite their diverse approaches to leadership.

Simply stated, *emotional intelligence* is a potent combination of self-management skills and the ability to collaborate with others. Studies at Yale University as well as the seminal work of Harvard psychologist, Daniel Goleman, all seem to point to five key characteristics of emotional intelligence:

- ✓ Knowing and understanding your emotions.
- ✓ Learning how to manage your emotions.
- ✓ Applying the principles of self-motivation to personal growth and development.
- ✓ Recognizing and understanding emotions in others.
- ✓ Managing relationships effectively.

In one of Daniel Goleman's cornerstone studies on emotional intelligence, he examined 188 largely global companies. The purpose of his research was to determine which personal competencies drove outstanding performance within those organizations. His study included three categories of competencies:

1. Purely technical skills, like X-ray technology or business accounting.
2. Cognitive abilities, such as deductive reasoning.
3. Competencies illustrating emotional intelligence, such as the ability to work well with a team.

"When I analyzed all of this data," Goleman concluded, "I found dramatic results. To be sure, intelligence was a driver of outstanding performance. Cognitive skills such as big-picture thinking and long-term vision were particularly important. But when I calculated the rates of technical skills, IQ, and emotional intelligence as ingredients of excellent performance, emotional intelligence proved to be twice as important as the others for jobs at all levels."

Goleman went on to say that emotional intelligence assumed an even more important role at the highest levels of the organization, where differences in people's technical and cognitive abilities were negligible.

When we examine the five characteristics of emotional intelligence, it will become evident how each one fosters high levels of employee engagement.

Knowing and Understanding Your Emotions

How engaged do you think employees would be at work if their manager routinely rode an emotional roller-coaster in one-on-one or team meetings? Leaders whose emotions are inconsistent typically foster tension, fear, and disengagement.

Several years ago I worked with the director of a hospital laboratory (we'll call him Bob) who had just lost his job. He was in shock after the termination because he'd always been told he was one of the brightest administrators. But the hospital let him go because the turnover rate in his department was twice the average of the other departments, and morale in the lab was at its lowest point in five years.

In fact, Bob was fired because he didn't know or understand how much the emotion of fear was destroying his leadership.

When I spoke with Bob, he said he had been afraid of losing his job ever since he started working at the hospital. It had been his first leadership role in any organization, and he thought that if he and his team members could do everything perfectly, the payoff would be job security. As a result, Bob micromanaged the department to death and his team members distanced themselves from him. Not even the Vice Presidents or the CEO really knew what was happening.

Bob's fear ultimately cost him his job. Why? Because it prevented him from genuinely engaging his people and becoming an effective coach to the people under his supervision. "Coaching" for Bob meant over-controlling and stifling the creativity and enthusiasm of his staff.

While Bob's story is disappointing, it is a clear example of how critical it is to know and to understand your emotions as a leader and how those emotions can facilitate employee engagement.

Learning How to Manage Your Emotions

It's one thing to know and understand your emotions; it's quite another to manage them effectively. To better understand this transition, think of the angry samurai who got in the face of his Zen master and challenged him to explain the meaning of heaven and hell.

With a condescending tone the Zen master said, "You're nothing but a moron, and I can't waste my time with an idiot like you." When he heard his character being assassinated, the samurai flew into a rage, drew his sword, and shouted, "I could kill you for your disrespect." In a very gentle and unassuming voice, the monk said, "That is hell."

Amazed at the wisdom of the Zen master and knowing that he had been possessed by a violent rage, the samurai immediately stepped back, put away his sword, and thanked the master for his insights as he bowed before him. "And that," the monk replied in the same unassuming and gentle voice, "is heaven."

Learning how to manage your emotions doesn't mean finding a way to repress them. Rather, managing your emotions in a coaching capacity means using them constructively to engage your team members and to bring out the best in them.

Whether you are in an individual or a group setting, you can assume one of three emotional positions in life, and two of them have the potential to destroy any hope for employee engagement.

Emotional position #1: I will act the way I feel. Choose this position when you're having a bad day and your results will be no better than the samurai's. In this position, emotions rule — and if the emotion is anger, resentment, impatience, fear, or frustration, odds are you'll do some damage with your words and actions and create some casualties among your team members.

Emotional position #2: You will act the way I feel. Your emotions are still in control here, but in this position you choose to make others feel as miserable as you do. "I'm upset so you should be upset too!" is what I heard one manager tell an employee in an automobile dealership recently. Having your team members feel as miserable as you do is completely counterproductive.

Emotional position #3: I can't help the way I feel right now, but I can help the way I think and act. This position is the very best blend of your three greatest resources as a leader: your intellect, your emotions, and your will. If your employees perform poorly during a business presentation, you could let your thinking and feelings unfold like this: "I'm so frustrated and angry with what I am hearing and seeing. But working myself into a frenzy now accomplishes nothing. What I need to do is express my concerns, redirect the group, and take steps to avoid a similar occurrence in the future." Integrating this third emotional position into your overall leadership style will greatly enhance your credibility and effectiveness as a coach.

Is it OK for you to use the first two emotional positions in certain situations? If you're passionate, enthusiastic, and hopeful and you're naturally expressing positive emotions, then act the way you feel and encourage others to do the same. The third emotional position, however, must be your guide when there is a clear and present danger of anger, frustration, cynicism, or other emotions that can destroy what is good in a team member, the entire team, or the overall work environment.

Applying the Principles of Self-Motivation

Motivation is one of the misunderstood words in the English language. But it is essential for you to comprehend the emotional intelligence aspects of motivation if you want to be a leader that effectively engages others.

To be a successful leader, you first need to have a passion for the mission of your company or organization. Motivating yourself towards achievement and measurable accomplishments sets an example and establishes performance expectations for your team members. In addition, your example invites them to engage you in a manner that generates collaboration, commitment, and cooperation. Self-motivated leaders are always looking for ways to improve. As a result, the team members they work with experience this passionate drive and get excited about learning, growing, and developing in their careers as well.

Someone once asked me, "Isn't getting employees engaged just about motivating them?" Not exactly! Getting co-workers engaged in the workplace involves creating that *learning, growing, and developing* environment for the purpose of helping them to discover and experience *meaning* in what they do, thereby enhancing both their professional skills and personal satisfaction.

So creating an engaged workplace implies a lot more than just motivation—though it's important to remember that motivation is a key tool that you can employ in the engagement process. To preserve your integrity as a leader, however, it is imperative that you be a model of self-motivation before you use motivation as a tool to inspire an engaged work team.

The reality is that motivation as an engagement resource can backfire pretty quickly when leaders lack awareness of what I have come to understand as the *Four Laws of Motivation* as described by psychologist Denis Waitley.

The Four Laws of Motivation

1. **You can't motivate anyone.** Human beings have intellects, emotions, and wills. And because of these three powerful influencers, most people willingly exercise their capacity to make hundreds of choices every day about what to think, feel, and do—without the benefit of a motivational crutch. Have you ever attended a multi-level marketing meeting where an energetic keynote speaker jumps up and down telling the screaming, enthusiastic participants that they can become millionaires? The people leave the meeting with excitement and conviction—but how many of them in fact become wealthy? Research tells us that the number is less than one percent. Why? The answer lies in the second law of motivation...

2. **All people are motivated.** Suppose two employees have the opportunity to take a class that will help them advance in their careers. One of them registers for the class; the other does not. What can we conclude? Simple. Given a similar set of circumstances for taking the class or not, one person was motivated to sign up while the other employee was motivated, for whatever reasons, to make a different choice. Motivation was a factor in both instances.

3. **People do things for their reasons, not yours.** Great parents and grandparents understand this law more than anyone. Because they have been gifted with intellects, emotions and wills, kids do things for their reasons, not yours. Employees aren't any different. And as much as we would like to think that we are ultimately responsible when our team members make great choices at work, that isn't the case. As a leader, I may have two or three reasons why a task needs to be accomplished a certain way to achieve a favorable result. My employee, however, may have two or three reasons why the task needs to be undertaken in a different manner to accomplish the same result. One of the keys to engaging employees successfully is to discern their wants and needs, gifts and talents, strengths and challenges, and then create an environment where they have the freedom and creativity to achieve the goals that you and the team have agreed upon.

4. **What we identify as a person's weakness is very often just an overextended strength.** Since this fourth law of motivation is the hardest one to master, permit me to share a work-related example. A friend of mine who is a company president called me one day to vent his exasperation with his relatively

new administrative assistant. "She's too slow making decisions when I'm not around," he blurted out. "She's been here six months and the smart, intelligent person I thought I had hired is forever mired in analysis paralysis. She needs me to decide on even the most minor issues. I'm thinking of terminating her employment on Monday, but I thought I would ask you if you thought there was any hope." I asked to meet with her for an hour. It was evident when we sat down to chat that Brenda was a bright, gifted, talented individual. So why wouldn't she make decisions when my friend Terry wasn't around?

As I spoke with Brenda, it became clear that her former boss had never allowed her to make any decision when he was not in the office — a behavior that actually contributed to her seeking new employment. Terry had labeled her as someone who wasn't capable of making a decision when, in fact, she hadn't reconciled the restrictive environment of her immediate past with Terry's need for a decision-maker in his absence.

In a short time, Terry realized that Brenda's overextended strength was that she followed directions to the letter. She simply had not put into perspective the directive of her former boss to never make a decision in his absence. Within a few weeks, everything worked out and Terry was a happy camper again. But his initial frustration was a microcosm of one of the most intense challenges you'll face in engaging your team members: not dwelling on their perceived weaknesses; rather, identifying and building upon their not-always-so-obvious strengths and talents.

Recognizing and Understanding Emotions in Others

This fundamental component of emotional intelligence is all about empathy. But let's not kid ourselves. When is the last time you heard of anyone being recognized for their empathy at work? The concept of empathy seems out of place in an economy where profit is king. But as a leader, empathy will be one of your most valuable tools in creating an engaged workforce.

When you're trying to create an environment where employees are locked into your business mission and supportive of one another, it's helpful to see their everyday responsibilities and tasks from their point of view — **before** you offer them any guidance or direction. The timeworn challenge to "walk a mile in my shoes" is sage advice to heed if leaders are to be viewed as credible and trustworthy.

At St. Elizabeth Medical Center in Utica, New York, I spoke with a Registered Nurse who had been on the staff for twenty-five years. She shared with me the main reason for her serving in one place for a quarter-century.

> "I think I was in my third or fourth month of employment here, and I was having a hard time balancing what I had learned in nursing school from the theoretical standpoint with the expectations and demands of real-time patient care. My supervisor at that time sensed that I was a little lost and frustrated. So she had lunch with me one day, and we had the greatest conversation about her beginnings in the nursing profession and the anxieties she felt.

Maybe a week later, she asked if she could work with me on the floor for a half-shift and share some insights. There's no question that her willingness to reach out to me when I needed help was directly responsible for me devoting my entire career to this medical center."

This nurse's story is a superb example of how empathy can have a significant impact on the careers of your team members.

Managing Relationships Effectively

The final component of emotional intelligence is being able to manage relationships effectively.

It would be totally naïve to suggest that *managing relationships effectively* simply means being friendly and helpful at work. Nor does it suggest that a leader merely walk through the halls, pat your team members on the back, and tell them what a great job they're doing.

Managing relationships effectively means moving people in the direction of accomplishing their personal, professional, and team goals. If customer satisfaction scores are low, for example, the leader guides the team in the direction of continuous improvement. If one of their team members is experiencing job-related difficulties, the leader facilitates solutions to whatever obstacles are impeding success.

Managing relationships effectively is the most visible result of emotional intelligence in the workplace. Your successful work with teams, for example, is evidence that you have mastered the skill of empathy. Your persuasive skills as a leader are testimony to your ability to earn the respect and trust of those whom you lead.

If you have developed a high level of emotional intelligence, relationships will be managed effectively because you will remain in an adult-to-adult frame of mind. Your communication with others will never resort to parental directives or childish rants. And you will seldom, if ever, be trapped in the vicious triangle of persecutor-rescuer-victim relationships.

Maybe you're not buying any of this emotional intelligence thinking just yet. That's not unusual. When I'm presenting seminars on employee engagement and managing relationships effectively, I'm always waiting for the inevitable question from a skeptic in the audience. It happened in Detroit a few years back when a senior-level manager stood up and asked, "It seems to me that all of this engagement stuff won't help me balance my budget. And as far as emotional intelligence is concerned, do you think that really matters when it comes to bottom-line profits?"

There is so much research on the importance of Emotional Intelligence (EQ), that I try to have a few studies on hand for questions like I received in Motor City. In response to his question, I briefly shared the following information:

The Carnegie Institute of Technology conducted research revealing that <u>85% of our financial success</u> was credited to skills in "human engineering," personality, and the ability to communicate, negotiate, and lead. They reported that only 15% was due to technical ability. In other words, people skills or skills highly related to emotional intelligence were crucial skills. Nobel Prize winning Israeli-American psychologist Daniel Kahneman found that people would rather do business with a person they like and trust rather than someone they don't, even if that person is offering a better product at a lower price.

Whatever the business environment, the case for creating employee engagement by developing the emotional intelligence of organizational leaders first, and then all employees, is compelling.

COACHING

Business coaching is attracting America's top CEOs because, put simply, business coaching works. In fact, when asked for a conservative estimate of monetary payoff from the coaching they got... managers described an average return of more than $100,000, or about six times what the coaching had cost their companies.

FORTUNE Magazine

The second foundational element of a highly engaged workplace culture is coaching. What successful coach recruits a team, hands each player the playbook, and then sits back and waits for them to execute the game plan? To develop a highly engaged workplace today, the mandate for contemporary leaders is to be heavily involved in coaching their employees to personal and professional success.

When I hear the term "coach," I take myself back to elementary school where Mrs. Moore was my 5th grade teacher. She did all of the typical things teachers do — instructed the students, assigned homework, and graded tests and quizzes. Today, while I remember Mrs. Moore as a teacher, I think of her now more as a coach.

Mrs. Moore was adept at using her emotional intelligence (a term that wasn't even in vogue then) to make sure her students received quality, one-on-one time with her. She was terrific when it came to focusing on the positive, identifying challenges, and helping to find solutions to problems. Mrs. Moore knew about your family, your strengths and weaknesses, and even your pet peeves. Making you feel like an important part of her class was a unique gift of Mrs. Moore. She could sense when you were having a good day or bad day, and she had a sense for what to say to you on both occasions.

While I loved being in Mrs. Moore's class, I never really appreciated her until many years later. She exemplified many of the very best coaching behaviors.

Since my days in the fifth grade, emotional intelligence has fueled coaching as a tool for improving personal and organizational performance. Actually, the practice of coaching as it relates to the workplace, is still a relatively new phenomenon although coaching others in one form or another has been an integral part of our culture for centuries.

Prior to reviewing the importance of coaching as it relates to employee engagement, it would be wise to dispel some of the common myths people hold about the role of coaching in the workplace.

The Top Five Coaching Myths

Coaching cannot be accurately defined. The reality: Coaching is a partnership between a leader and a team member characterized by two commitments. The leader commits to fostering an environment where each team member has an opportunity to learn, to grow, and to develop in their career. In similar fashion, the team member commits to the development and implementation of a coaching plan in conjunction with his or her team leader. The coaching plan identifies specific action steps that will be taken by the team member and supported by the team leader for the purpose of achieving personal and professional job satisfaction, career development goals, and buy-in to the company's mission, values, business goals and objectives.

Some people just can't be coached. The reality: Any team member can be coached for performance improvement if he or she has an open mind or a willingness to learn, grow, and change.

Coaching is like mental health therapy. The reality: Nothing could be further from the truth. While coaching requires a certain level of emotional intelligence, the goals of a coaching process in the workplace are quite different from the goals of individual therapy.

A coach is nothing more than a cheerleader. The reality: Cheerleaders have rah-rah pep rallies and root the team to victory. Coaches prepare the team, develop the team's talent, and capitalize on each person's individual strengths while creating a commitment to team goals.

Coaching has nothing to do with service, outcomes, and cost. The reality: Improved morale, lower employee turnover, and better teamwork all have a significant impact on the organization's bottom-line. Coaching affects all three measures.

Actually, the top five myths could easily become the top twenty-five in a discussion about the misconceptions people have about coaching employees in the workplace. Perhaps the one fallacy pervading most discussions about coaching is that the coaching process is always a part of some disciplinary action. Often, coaching is perceived as the first step of a very unpleasant three-step journey — coaching, counseling, and finally, termination. Coaching intended to achieve higher levels of employee engagement is founded upon a more positive and productive intent— namely, to help employees to learn, grow, and develop in their jobs and careers, thereby enhancing both their professional skills and personal satisfaction, all the while generating a passionate, driving force to achieve the mission and objectives of the business.

When I was developing a leadership development initiative for a southeastern utility, I met a technician who couldn't say enough good things about her supervisor. The technician had worked at the utility for about seven years. It was her first job after high school and some technical training.

The technician's name was Melanie and in an employee focus group I conducted, she offered this:

> "When I came here I was really scared. I was afraid to make a mistake, and there were so many people telling me what to do and not to do after my employee orientation that I was confused. I decided my team leader was very approachable, and she seemed both genuinely interested in both my career and me. I trusted her to help me. She did. And today I'm a better person and technician as a result of the trust I placed in her."

Melanie's story reflects the perfect outcome of a coaching relationship that drives powerful employee engagement: the development of a long-term, dedicated employee who is professionally competent and who feels valued by her team leader and her employer. It's an outcome that just didn't happen mysteriously; it was the result of that leader exercising her responsibilities as a coach and building a meaningful relationship with her team member.

When leaders become coaches to their employees, the result is high level employee engagement at every organizational level. And in essence, every good coach has five essential coaching responsibilities:

The coach is responsible for creating a work environment where employees can learn, grow, and develop — and thereby enhance their professional skills and personal job satisfaction.

The coach is responsible for building a collaborative coaching relationship — based upon mutual trust and open communication.

The coach is responsible for thoroughly understanding the characters and competencies of team members so that he/she can guide those employees to higher levels of professional engagement and personal enrichment.

The coach is responsible for applying the principles of emotional intelligence and employing core coaching competencies to maximize his/her effectiveness in the coaching relationship.

The coach is responsible for developing his/her team members' belief in the value of the coaching relationship. As this belief is strengthened, each team member will feel more comfortable sharing his/her knowledge, skills, and abilities with both the coach and with fellow team members.

Sound like a lot of work? It is. But the end result of the commitment to coaching yields benefits that spark innovation, creativity, and a highly collaborative work group. In a focus group that I conducted among employees at an automobile manufacturer where emotionally intelligent coaching drove operations at every level of the company, a cross-section of employees listed these outcomes:

- ✓ Improved team member satisfaction.
- ✓ Advanced the education and careers of team members.
- ✓ Increased productivity through the accomplishment of personal and team goals.
- ✓ Enhanced leadership skills.
- ✓ The generation of new ideas to benefit the entire company.
- ✓ The destruction of relationship barriers that prohibit effective communication.
- ✓ Identification of future leaders through the coaching process.
- ✓ The retention of valued team members.
- ✓ Increased customer satisfaction.

Yes, coaching is the hard work of a highly successful leader. But as you can see from the random sample of results identified by a group of engaged co-workers, the expected outcomes certainly justify the efforts expended to achieve them.

Implementing an effective coaching process is without question one of the most important things an organization can do to ensure the personal and professional development of its team members, and thereby accomplish its mission and objectives.

Of fundamental importance is the basic reality that coaching is about relationship building. When the leader-employee relationship is strong, the resulting benefits include higher levels of engagement and morale, improved performance, and maximized organizational effectiveness. That's why it was imperative to establish emotional intelligence and understanding the person within as the foundation for employee engagement. Knowing yourself as a person and understanding your coaching character is the initial step in building strong coaching relationships with the members of your team or department.

At a manufacturing organization in the southeast where I did some work in recent years, one of the supervisors in my training session was a very bottom-line type of individual. During an afternoon break, she approached me with this request: "I'm a big believer in the necessity and effectiveness of coaching. And I believe that the information and tools we're acquiring today will be very helpful. But can you put all of this into a simple, sound, step-by-step formula that I can remember to use every day, without having to reference a book or a binder?"

It was the best question posed by anyone that day and, thankfully, I had tested and proven the formula that the supervisor requested.

The Coaching Relationship Cycle

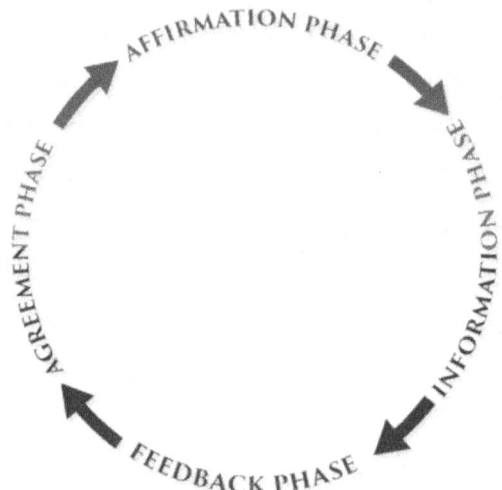

Because the work of coaching implies a process of relationship-building as noted earlier, it is best accomplished in the following four distinct phases. As you develop your coaching skills, you will find that the phases of *Affirmation, Information, Feedback, and Agreement* combine to form an easy-to-remember and practically applied approach to any coaching transaction. Moreover, you will also discover that these phases foster an environment characterized by a candor and openness that forms a solid foundation for an engaged coaching relationship.

The Affirmation Phase

The first phase of the coaching relationship cycle is the *affirmation phase*. The word *affirmation*, as applied in the coaching context, signifies that leaders affirm the character, competence, and career of each employee that they are coaching.

Looking for a way to kick off the affirmation phase on the wrong foot? Approach one of your employees and say, "Carol, those reports you've been sending me aren't written very effectively." Comments like this guarantee a failing grade in Counseling 101 and only serve to alienate rather than engage your team member.

So maybe this person's reports are in need of improvement. Affirmation, not accusation, is the best way to effect meaningful change over time. How about this? "Carol, I really appreciate the reports you've been sending me. I know those reports are just one more thing you have to do in your hectic schedule. If you could meet with me tomorrow for about ten minutes, I would like to hear your ideas and suggest some of my own for streamlining those reports in a way that you could save us both some valuable time. Would morning or afternoon work best for you?

If you as a leader are genuinely interested in facilitating Carol's engagement at work, then affirming her diligence in sending the reports and offering to work with her to improve their effectiveness yields the best results. Merely telling her that she's prepared the reports inefficiently does nothing but create anger, resentment, and frustration while contributing absolutely nothing to boosting her self-esteem.

The Information Phase

Once you have a firm grip on the *affirmation phase* of the coaching relationship cycle, you can then proceed to the *information phase*. The information phase consists of adult-to-adult dialogue between you and each of your employees so that, partnering with them, you can focus on their personal and professional growth and development.

Interaction in this phase can occur at any time, and it's not limited to a structured coaching session. Your role as a leader at this juncture is to create opportunities for each of your employees to enhance their individual talents and professional competencies while at the same time contributing to the strength of the team.

The primary tool employed during the information phase is communication. Communication is to the information phase what blood is to the body — if the flow of meaningful communication doesn't exist, then an inevitable disconnect occurs between you and your team member(s).

Some time ago I met Wilson, a very talented, yet disgruntled salesperson. Wilson's department manager approached him during the week with these instructions: "There's a sales class next week that I think would be good for you to attend. Here's the brochure. Let me know how it goes."

Wilson went on to share with me that it was customary for him to receive "orders" like this with little follow-up from his manager. When I asked him what he would do differently if he was the one in charge and I was the salesperson, Wilson said he would approach me with a conversation like this:

> "Tom, I really appreciate the work you're doing in my department. What I'm trying to do is to find materials and programs that I believe would help you develop skills that will advance your career. I found a seminar next week that I think will interest you, one that will enable you to make an even greater contribution to our department. I will help you to adjust your work schedule if you'd like to attend. And after you have

participated in the sales training, I would like to sit down with you and find out how you think what you have learned might benefit our team. How does that sound to you?"

In listening to Wilson's approach, I wasn't surprised that he began the conversation by valuing my contribution to the department and then seeking to establish a collaborative connection that would fuel my desire for career growth and development. He was simply treating me the way he wanted to be treated.

In the information phase, it doesn't matter **what** information you need to exchange with each one of your team members; the essential factor is **how** you share that information. And because communication is so essential in this phase, it is important to be aware of and to employ effective communication techniques so that both your formal coaching sessions and informal one-to-one interactions are worthwhile and productive.

In each of your coaching relationships, use the following suggestions to guarantee that the information phase achieves its intended results:

- ✓ Make no assumption that a team member you are coaching has actually understood what you've had to say. Ask point-blank if you have communicated everything clearly.
- ✓ Be honest, direct, and compassionate when you communicate with your team members. In the workplace, where time and integrity are both at a premium, there is no room for disingenuous communication.

- ✓ Be assertive but not aggressive. Assertiveness leaves no doubt about what you are saying in the mind of the listener; conversely, aggression almost always results in defensiveness.
- ✓ Create a work atmosphere that invites communication. Make it a point to actively seek out the facts, opinions, and ideas of others.
- ✓ Be non-judgmental in your communications.
- ✓ People communicate on four basic levels: facts, feelings, values, and opinions. Understanding the differences among those levels promotes healthy dialogue.
- ✓ Avoid win-lose and "I'm right, you're wrong" communication scenarios. Being willing and able to compromise ensures healthy communication between you and your team members.
- ✓ Demonstrate respect for yourself and your team members at all times. By dignifying the worth of every team member, you create an environment where mutual trust and respect become the cornerstone of effective communication.
- ✓ Own your communication and be responsible for your feelings. Using "I" statements rather than "he," "she," "you," or "it" statements is much more effective when personal responsibility and credibility are at stake.
- ✓ Seek first to understand, then to be understood. A little empathy goes a long way toward establishing a rapport with your team members that is helpful and productive.

The Feedback Phase

While the information phase is founded upon effective communication, the leader who masters the feedback phase of the coaching relationship cycle is one who employs legendary listening skills. The feedback phase is essential because it gives all employees an opportunity to clarify a plan of action, ask questions, or to state their opinions about a particular issue.

Contemporary research is clear that employees seldom quit their **jobs**; more often, they quit their **bosses**. In exit interviews I've conducted with departing employees from a variety of organizations, there is one recurrent, discouraging theme: *I left because my supervisor never listened to me.* This shouldn't surprise anyone. Many years ago at the University of Minnesota, two courses were offered: one in communication and the other in listening. So many people registered for the communication course that the university had to add two additional sections.

The listening class, however, was cancelled because no one registered for it. Everybody wanted to learn how to talk; no one wanted to learn how to listen.

If you're like most managers, you've received little or no training on how to listen effectively. You've probably been conditioned to simply disseminate information while focusing on objectives and outcomes. And the volume of work you face can pressure you to depersonalize the work environment in favor of time and expedience. Big mistake.

Creating a forum for feedback from your team members is critical to engaging employees and developing a coaching relationship with them. Here are some tips for enhancing your listening skills:

- ✓ Listen to your employees and co-workers openly and empathetically. When you try to see things from their perspective, you will foster a climate of cooperation and collaboration.

- ✓ When communication requires follow-up, make sure you and your colleague decide immediately upon specific follow-up actions and plans.
- ✓ When you're speaking with one of your team members, reflect back to him/her what you think you have heard. It's the very best way to overcome serious pitfalls in listening.
- ✓ If a team member's communication with you is detailed, take notes or do whatever else is necessary to accurately record the conversation.
- ✓ Don't let distractions like phone calls, pagers, and email arrivals interrupt your communication with one of your team members.
- ✓ Not everyone may communicate as well as you do. So listen with patience and understanding — every time.
- ✓ Listen to your team members with interest, and let them know you understand what they've told you.
- ✓ Look for nonverbal cues while you're listening. A person's body language, for example, can tell you a lot about what they're trying to say.
- ✓ Ask for as much detail as the person you're speaking with can provide, and make sure you have a good understanding of the facts before responding.
- ✓ Don't shoot the messenger! When you react to what you hear, make certain you separate the content of the message from the person delivering it.

The Agreement Phase

If the coaching process that fosters employee engagement was to stop here without moving to the fourth phase, it might produce a few temporary benefits, but nothing of substance in the long run. The *affirmation, information*, and *feedback* phases of the coaching cycle cannot survive alone. They need the *agreement* phase to ensure personal and professional growth and development among the members of your team.

The purpose of the agreement phase is to bring to fruition what you have affirmed, communicated, and discussed with one of your team members. It's a consensus-seeking phase that results in a decision to act in some capacity. Suppose, for instance, that Monica approaches me, her team leader, with some obstacles that she is experiencing with computers and information technology. I reassure her that she has the ability to overcome these obstacles and, after listening to her issues and concerns, I suggest some training that could be of help to her. Monica gives me some feedback about the proposed training and suggests that she also be allowed to partner with another team member who is proficient in the IT area. We then spend some time working out the logistics of the training that may impact her departmental responsibilities.

What's next? The agreement phase — a commitment to action and follow-up.

> "Monica, these classes are scheduled at different times over the next two months. Can you let me know by Monday which class you plan to take, and also when you will be working with Mary from IT? I think your

idea to work with her after the class will be a great way to combine the information you will learn in the class with the practical experience she will be able to share with you."

The cornerstone of the agreement phase is a collaborative commitment to action. If it is important to your company to engage your employees in the workplace, then you and your team members are compelled to take whatever steps are necessary in order to make that engagement possible and real.

The agreement phase is the litmus test of the coaching relationship cycle. When you as a coach have done your homework in the affirmation, information, and feedback phases, the agreement phase delivers the results you desire from your coaching relationships with your colleagues. Each of your team members makes a personal commitment to engage with you as they learn, grow, and develop. You, as a leader and coach, become an enduring catalyst for each person's long-term career development within your organization.

Remember the question posed to me by the manufacturing supervisor who attended my training seminar in Florida? *But can you put all of this into a simple and sound step-by-step formula I can remember to use every day without having to consult a book or a binder?* Of course, here's the formula:

AFFIRMATION + INFORMATION + FEEDBACK + AGREEMENT =
EMPLOYEE ENGAGEMENT & SUSTAINABLE COMPETITIVE ADVANTAGE

The Employee Engagement Challenge

When people are financially invested, they want a return. When people are emotionally invested, they want to contribute.

Simon Sinek

Talk is cheap when it comes to creating a highly energized and engaged work environment. The fact is that too few companies understand the power of passionate people at work. In addition, *emotional intelligence* and *coaching* skills are seldom priorities when it comes to recruiting, selecting, hiring, and training business leaders.

So cutting to the bottom line, what are the things your company needs to do in order to achieve maximum and sustainable levels of employee engagement? Here's the checklist:

1. The most important pre-requisite for a highly engaged workforce is a C.E.O./Board of Directors that understands, embraces, and supports in every way possible — programs, policies, procedures, and processes designed to make engagement a top organizational priority. If your company doesn't have that kind of support, don't waste your time.

2. Without emotionally intelligent people that know how to coach and be coached, engagement doesn't happen. Make certain that the end result of your hiring process is the acquisition of that type of talent.

3. Engaged workplaces have leaders that know how to manage, not managers who are clueless in the leadership category. In addition, engaged leaders understand the difference between power and authority; they have power by virtue of their job title, but zero authority unless it is given to them by their employees. Routinely assess your leadership with 360-degree feedback tools.

4. Create effective feedback channels to ensure that communication in your company is a two-way street. Listening to your people is an essential element of an engaged work environment. Annual surveys, regular department meetings, daily stand-up sessions, and interactive employee information platforms are just a few suggestions for maintaining open communication.

5. An absolute essential for engaged employees is a personal growth and development plan (PGDP) that is reviewed with the employee at least annually. If you want your employees to feel as though they have a future with your company, the PGDP lays out a roadmap for how to achieve their personal and professional development goals. A PGDP is not a performance review and has nothing to do with wages or salary. It

is a tool for both leaders and employees to create a path for growth and development within the company.

6. In conducting exit interviews with disengaged employees who left their employment, money is typically identified as one of the primary reasons for their departure. It might surprise some to know, however, that one of the other top reasons for leaving is a lack of training. "They never taught me anything," one disgruntled ex-employee offered. "That's how I knew they didn't care about me." If you're going to hire someone, have the common sense to teach them how to do their job and then provide ongoing training to enhance their skills.

7. This is the first time in our nation's history where we may find five different generations of employees working within the same department. And every generation has a unique way of learning, communicating, and performing in the workplace. In addition, we work in an era where we have the benefit of multi-cultural talents in our pool of organizational resources. Leaders who want to fully engage a multi-generational and multi-cultural workforce require special training in how to accomplish that task.

8. If the goal of a company is to create high-performing work teams, then understanding the four essential elements of team performance is imperative. An NFL quarterback doesn't get asked to help the team by playing a defensive lineman's position. Most certainly, that would be a disaster. In similar fashion, eleven wide-receivers can't all play offense at the same time.

Every company has people with one or more primary team skill sets: some are gifted when it comes to creating ideas; others are more inclined to take an idea and advance it to the next level of development; a third personality type enjoys the devil's advocate role and refines the idea to ensure its workability; finally, the executors on the team make sure that the idea/project gets implemented successfully. High levels of employee engagement are obtained when a healthy balance of work styles are assigned to undertake work projects.

9. Don't underestimate the importance of well-constructed employee recognition programs. As much as some will deny it, it's human nature to take personal satisfaction in being appreciated for what we accomplish. Especially for those that have gone above and beyond what was expected of them, meaningful (that's the key word) recognition efforts can instill pride, camaraderie, and teamwork in your organization.

10. The final point on the checklist is the hardest to accomplish. A primary goal of a great leader is to nurture and to develop other great leaders. I want the people that work with me to know and understand as much as or more about the job than I do. An ill-advised manager in a utility company that I consulted with said, "I don't know what my people would do without me. I need to watch over them every step of the way." My company doesn't need sheep in search of a shepherd. I want people that have a desire to lead with their unique gifts and talents. Make certain that you've hired leaders in your

company who understand that their primary role is to coach and to develop other great leaders.

Achieving high levels of employee engagement isn't easy, but it's not rocket science either. Using the tools of emotional intelligence and coaching, any organization can reach a level of performance where a passionate, engaged workforce accomplishes the mission of a company dedicated to serving its employees as well as its customers.

ABOUT THE AUTHORS

Tom McQueen

Tom McQueen is an award-winning author, executive coach, and Vice President of *It's Just Common Sense, Inc*.

His current and former clients include the Penske Automotive Group, BayCare Health System, Gulf Power Company, the City of Pensacola, and the Tampa Bay Rays.

Serving God and community is a passion of Tom's. His presentation on *Faith, Family & Miracles* receives rave reviews in churches throughout the United States and Canada. Tom also serves as a Fire Commissioner for the East Lake Tarpon Special Fire Control District in Palm Harbor, Florida.

Karl Horst

Major General Karl Horst retired from the United States Army on October 1, 2013 after four decades of enlisted and commissioned service. During that time, he had the privilege to lead Soldiers at every level of the military, at home and around the world, in peacetime and in combat.

After his retirement from active duty, and following a non-traditional path of many retired general officers, Karl entered the automobile industry. His first responsibility was as a leadership trainer and consultant, but he then transitioned to leading a major automotive manufacturer line as a General Sales Manager, eventually becoming the General Manager of a dealership.

Karl now lectures on "Common Sense Leadership," and "Leading Change in Large Organizations." As the founder of *It's Just Common Sense, LLC,* he and his team consult and partner with businesses to implement a holistic process to develop people and productivity by engaging employees in business goals and objectives.

Karl is a graduate of the National Automotive Dealers Association (NADA) Dealer Academy and attended the University of North Carolina Kenan-Flagler Business School Executive Development Program. He received his bachelor's degree from the United States Military Academy at West Point and a master's degree in Public Administration from Shippensburg University of Pennsylvania. He is also a graduate of the U.S. Army War College.

During his time on active duty, Karl received numerous awards and decorations including two awards of the Distinguished Service Medal, two awards of the Defense Superior Service Medal, five awards of the Legion of Merit, three awards of the Bronze Star Medal, and the French Ordre National du Mérite. Additionally, he is a Combat Infantryman, a Master Parachutist, and an Army Ranger. His travels include six continents and 65 different countries throughout the world.

About the Authors

Karl resides in Tampa Florida with his wife of more than 34 years, Nancy. They have three grown children and three grandchildren.

www.ingramcontent.com/pod-product-compliance
Lightning Source LLC
Chambersburg PA
CBHW061227180526
45170CB00003B/1196